D1569756

WE WERE HERE FIRST
THE NATIVE AMERICANS

THE
IROQUOIS
OF THE NORTHEAST

KaaVonia
Hinton

PURPLE TOAD
PUBLISHING

P.O. Box 631
Kennett Square, Pennsylvania 19348
www.purpletoadpublishing.com

WE WERE HERE FIRST
THE NATIVE AMERICANS

The Apache of the Southwest
The Inuit of the Arctic
The Iroquois of the Northeast
The Nez Perce of the Pacific Northwest
The Sioux of the Great Northern Plains

Printing   1   2   3   4   5   6   7   8   9

Publisher's Cataloging-in-Publication Data
Hinton, KaaVonia
   The Iroquois of the Northeast / KaaVonia
Hinton
      p. cm.—(We were here first: The Native
Americans)
   Includes bibliographic references and index.
      ISBN: 978-1-62469-079-2 (library bound)
1. Iroquois Indians—Juvenile literature.   I. Title.
                                    E99.I7 2013
                         974.70049755—dc23
                                     2013946334

eBook ISBN: 9781624690808

Printed by Lake Book Manufacturing, Chicago, IL

CONTENTS

Hiawatha was the first warrior to accept the Peacemaker's message. Together, they encouraged nations to live peacefully.

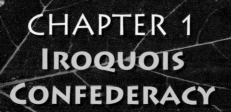

CHAPTER 1
IROQUOIS
CONFEDERACY

Hiawatha grabbed his spear. His wife and daughters lay dying and someone had to pay. An Onondaga (ah-nen-DA-gah) warrior, Hiawatha was skilled at hunting down enemies and killing them. In time, killing became his way of life.

Hiawatha lived during the "dark times," a period when the five Iroquois (ear-uh-KWAH) nations were constantly at war with their enemies, the Huron and Algonquin-speaking Indians. The nations also fought each other.

The name "Iroquois" suggests that they were skilled fighters. The name given to them by Algonquin-speaking Indians was Hilokoa, or "Killer People."[1] Similarly, the Mohawks, one of the Iroquois nations, call themselves Ganiengehaka, or "People of the Flint Country." But because of their fierce fighting, their enemies called them *Mowak* (Mohawk), or "Man-eaters."[2] Many people were killed during the dark times. Something had to be done to stop the fighting.

As the legend goes, many years ago the Creator grew tired of the fighting. Neighbors were afraid of one another. He wanted the bloodshed to end. According to the story, the

This wampum belt illustrates the nations' union. The "Tree of Peace" in the center and each square symbolizes a nation: the Onondagas, Keepers of the Central Fire; the Mohawks, Keepers of the Eastern Door; the Oneidas; the Cayugas; and the Seneca, Keepers of the Western Door.

Creator sent Dekanawideh, or the Peacemaker, to tell the nations to be peaceful. The Peacemaker built a canoe out of stone and traveled to tell others to work toward peace. First he visited a woman named Jingosahseh and told her his dream of a Great Peace among the nations. Jingosahseh thought the Great Peace was a good idea. She became known as the Mother of Nations and helped the Peacemaker spread his message. The Peacemaker also talked to Hiawatha. Hiawatha found comfort in the Peacemaker's message. He put down his weapons and began to help the Peacemaker share news about the Great Peace. Hiawatha recorded the message using seashell beads called *wampum* that he wove into belts. The wampum would help others remember the story of peace.

Atotarho

The Peacemaker and Hiawatha often sought help and advice from Jingosahseh, the first clan mother.[3] They shared the message with the Mohawks, and theirs became the first nation to accept the message of peace. It took many years for the Peacemaker and Hiawatha to share the message with the other nations, but one by one, they all accepted it. Only one Onondaga man did not. His name was Atotarho. With a twisted body and snakes nesting in his hair, Atotarho did not think peace was a good idea. He refused to join the Peacemaker's mission to unite the nations.

The Peacemaker had an idea. He invited leaders of the nations to a special meeting. Once there, he told them to form a confederacy and unite the nations. Their government would have "trust, checks and balances, and compromise."[4]

The Peacemaker explained that the nations would no longer need to fight because the confederacy would solve problems by talking about them to create a solution. The nations would operate under a set of rules called the Great Law of Peace. Each nation would send chiefs to sit on the Grand Council. This important council would be the nation's government, said the Peacemaker. The Peacemaker told each nation to keep a fire burning in their village. He explained that although the Grand Council would be powerful, each nation would still be independent—and they would all obey the law.[5]

Since Atotarho did not agree with the Peacemaker's

The snake-haired Atotarho

idea, everyone visited him to explain how the Iroquois Confederacy would work. To make Atotarho more likely to agree, the Peacemaker said the Grand Council could meet on the land of Atotarho's nation, Onondaga land. The Peacemaker and Hiawatha sang songs of peace to Atotarho and combed the snakes from his hair. They healed his body and mind. Finally, Atotarho agreed. He eventually became a spiritual leader.

The Peacemaker dug up the Great Tree of Peace, buried their weapons, and said,

"Under the shade of this Tree of Peace . . . there shall you sit and watch the Fire of the League of Five Nations. Roots have spread out from the Tree of Great Peace. . . . These are the Great White Roots, and their nature is Peace and Strength. If any man or any nation shall obey the Laws of Peace . . . they may trace back the roots of the Tree. . . . They shall be welcomed to take shelter beneath the Great Evergreen Tree."[6]

The Tree of Peace

The tree was replanted on Onondaga land.

Haudenosaunee

Six different nations make up the Native American group we call the Iroquois. They are the Onondaga, Mohawk, Oneida (oh-NY-da), Seneca, Cayuga (ky-YOO-ga), and Tuscarora (Tus-ka-ROR-ah).

The Peacemaker held the first council meeting on Onondaga land. There, the nations formed the Iroquois Confederacy.

The Iroquois settled in the northeastern part of the United States in present-day New York State over a thousand years ago. Originally, there were five nations, but during the early 1700s, the Tuscarora, attacked by colonists, fled their home in North Carolina and joined the league of five nations in New York.[7]

The six nations are a part of a larger group of Iroquois-speaking Native Americans. The other nations are the Cherokee and Huron.[8] The six nations are unique because together they make up a government called the Iroquois Confederacy. The Iroquois call themselves Haudenosaunee (ho-den-oh-SAW-nee), or People of the Longhouse. They are connected by language, beliefs, and traditions.[9]

No one knows when the Iroquois Confederacy was created. The Seneca were the largest nation when the Confederacy began. For years,

The tribes that comprise the Iroquois

the Seneca passed on the story of their history to others. They explained that they adopted the Iroquois Great Law of Peace soon after a total eclipse of the sun.[10] Since this Iroquois legend, or myth, says a total eclipse of the sun took place during the Iroquois Confederacy, scholars believe the Iroquois Confederacy probably began in 1142, when there was a total eclipse over New York.[11]

Today, the Iroquois Confederacy has a Grand Council made up of fifty chiefs. Two tribes have nine chiefs at the Grand Council—the Mohawk and Oneida tribes. Ten chiefs are Cayuga, fourteen are Onondaga, and eight are Seneca. After the Tuscarora joined the original five nations, the Oneida handled their affairs at the Grand Council.[12]

Women did not speak at traditional council meetings.[13] Despite this, their voices were heard. In 1724, a priest named Joseph-François Lafitau said women had "all real authority" and were "the souls of the Councils, the [negotiators] of peace and war."[14]

The Iroquois Confederacy is a government separate from that of the United States or any other government. The Great Law of Peace led to the Cayugas, the Oneidas, the Onondagas, the Senecas, and the Tuscaroras becoming what may have been the most powerful and important group of American Indians in eastern North America during the eighteenth century.[15]

The Nations'
Iroquois Names

As shown in the map, several Indian nations lived along major waterways near the Iroquois Confederacy.

The Nations used descriptions of the locations of their homes or their customs to name themselves.[16]

Oneida   People of the Standing Stone, or Granite People

Mohawks   People of the Flint Country

Onondaga   People on the Hills

Seneca   Great Hill People

Cayuga   People of the Great Swamp

Tuscarora   Shirt Wearing People

Communities worked together to build longhouses and the palisades that protected them.

CHAPTER 2
COMMUNITY

The Iroquois settled in the northeastern part of what came to be the United States over a thousand years ago. Once in New York State, they built villages one to two miles inland to protect themselves from attacks by enemies such as the Huron and Algonquin-speaking Indians. Twenty-foot-tall fences called palisades surrounded villages and provided protection. Palisades had front and back entrances that could be closed quickly with logs if an enemy attacked. During wartime, scalps were hung on large poles along the fence to scare attackers. Sometimes the Iroquois dug ditches along the side of a palisade for additional protection from intruders.

Rivers and streams were always close by so the Iroquois could travel easily by water in canoes. Mohawks lived along the Mohawk River, and the Oneida along the Oneida Lake in modern-day Syracuse. Chittenango Falls were located near the Onondaga, the Cayuga relied on the Montezuma Marsh, and the Seneca had access to the Genesee River. The rivers provided food and water for the nations' villages.[1]

Villages varied in size. A small village might have a dozen homes in it. Larger villages of 1,000 people had as many as sixty houses and buildings. Villages had steam-bath huts, small houses for one or two families, and longhouses.[2]

Longhouses had many uses. Some were houses, while others served as hospitals, schools, and spiritual dwellings.

Longhouses were windowless homes made of wood. They were between 50 and 150 feet long.[3] Longhouses were communal; this means many families lived in the same longhouse. Some longhouses were large enough to hold twenty-four families, usually from the same clan. Families lived in small compartments within one longhouse. The longhouse held platforms that served as beds and seats. Cornhusks and blankets made from animal fur covered the platforms. Each family had a fire to use for cooking and warming their home. Women took care of the longhouse. The chief's longhouse was usually larger than the others. Meetings and feasts were held there.[4]

The nations also saw the longhouse as a symbol of where they lived on the land and how they were connected as a confederacy. In the symbolic longhouse, the Seneca were at its Western Door, the Mohawks were the Keepers of its Eastern Door, and the Onondaga were the Keepers of the Central Fire, because they lived in the heart of Iroquois country.[5] The Onondaga were the capital of the Haudenosaunee.[6] The Cayuga lived just west of the Onondaga and the Oneida were just to the east.[7]

Most modern Iroquois people do not live in longhouses, but they are still important places. Longhouses are now used for religious ceremonies.[8]

Clans

Family and community are very important to the Iroquois. Each person belongs to a clan. A clan is a group of families that trace their heritage through a shared female ancestor. Though everyone belongs to a clan, some clan members live in different villages and among different

As shown here, several families lived and worked together under one roof.

nations. For example, historically, a married man went to live in his wife's family's longhouse, and their children belonged to their mother's clan.[9]

Long ago, clan members were not allowed to marry each other because they were related. However, the Iroquois often adopted Indians from other nations, Europeans, and Africans who escaped from slavery.[10] Scholars say the Iroquois used war to acquire new clan members. When early Iroquois lost tribe members during war, they selected prisoners to take their places. They gave the prisoners the clan members' names and identities.[11]

A clan mother led each clan. She was the oldest and most respected woman of a family. Among early Iroquois, the clan mother led the longhouse where her family lived. Each clan also had chiefs. The clan mother was responsible for choosing the chiefs, and she could also remove them.[12]

A clan mother had other responsibilities, too. For instance, she named the children when they were born. Traditionally, nations did not give the same name to multiple children. Married women kept their own names. They did not take the names of their husbands, and children did not take their fathers' last names.[13]

Iroquois women grind corn and gather berries as a baby sleeps in a cradleboard

Clan Names

Several nations have turtle, wolf, and bear clans.

Clans were named after animals that provided "special assistance" to a nation.[14] Clans had an animal symbol that was usually carved above longhouses. Scholars say the clans are divided by sky, earth, and water. The six nations have nine clans. However, the number of clans in an individual nation varies.[15]

The Nations' Clans

Mohawk   Turtle, Wolf, and Bear

Oneida   Turtle, Wolf, and Bear

Cayuga   Bear, Heron, Snipe, Turtle, and Wolf

Onondaga   Turtle, Wolf, Bear, Snipe, Heron, Beaver, Deer, Eel, and Hawk

Seneca   Turtle, Wolf, Bear, Snipe, Heron, Beaver, Deer, and Hawk

During cold weather, warriors wore more clothing. This photograph shows two warriors wearing headdresses, leggings, and beaded moccasins.

CHAPTER 3
DAILY LIFE

Everyone in a village had important work to do. Women owned land, harvested crops, gathered firewood, took care of the children, and made household goods, such as mats, clothes, shoes, and pots.

They also created art, including woven baskets, embroidery, dolls, pottery, and hair ornaments.[1] Iroquois women decorated the clothes they made out of animal materials. European colonists introduced the Iroquois to calico and flannel cloth or fabric. The Iroquois used it to make clothes. Later, they wore European clothing that they decorated with beads, shells, porcupine quills, and feathers. Women wore petticoats, or slips, and blouses while men wore flannel and ruffled shirts.

Early Iroquois used timber, bark, and woody fibers to make household and hunting tools, such as wooden bowls, bows, and arrow shafts. The men built longhouses, palisades, canoes, and animal traps. They also grew tobacco and spent most of their time hunting, fishing, and engaging in battle.

Crops were also a major food source. Men cleared the fields, but women did all of the other farm work. Land within the village was divided into family plots where crops were grown, harvested, and shared with others in the village. If a family abandoned a piece of land, another family could claim it.[3]

This diorama shows how beans and squash sprout up beside the corn once it matures. This happens just in time for the Green Corn Festival, a celebration the Iroquois started in order to give thanks for the crops.

The Iroquois called corn, beans, and squash the Three Sisters. The Three Sisters were called Deohako (jo-HAY-ko), the life supporters.[4] First, the corn was planted. Once it sprouted, beans or squash seeds were planted beside it. This kept bean and squash vines off the ground, making it easier to keep weeds away from the crops.

A village stored crops in buildings that looked like longhouses. When possible, foods were dried. Corn was braided and hung about the longhouse.[5]

The Green Corn Festival was held to thank the Three Sisters after corn, beans, and squash became ripe.[6] The festival lasted for a few days. It included music, dancing, and games. Babies were also named during the festival.[7]

Beans were used in different recipes, including cornbread. The Iroquois also ate fruits, nuts, and berries. Corn was an important food cooked in many ways. It was baked, boiled, or mashed and used to make bread and cereal.

Aside from being a tasty ingredient in meals, corn had other uses. The cobs were used in fires to smoke meat and hides. Stalks were weapons for children who played war, while corn silk was used for cornhusk dolls.[8] Corn was also used to construct rattles the Iroquois used to make music. A rattle was created by putting dried corn kernels inside turtle shells, gourds, bison horns, or folded, dried bark.[9]

Hunting and Fishing

Hunters made sure the Iroquois community enjoyed a rich diet of deer, bear, beaver, squirrel, and rabbit.[10] Sometimes they hunted in large groups. They formed a V-shaped line and marched through the forest, with the hunters at the open ends of the V leading the way to drive

The Iroquois often hunted deer.

animals forward.[11] Hunters used good luck charms they believed had spirits that would help them hunt successfully.[12] While hunting was their main way of getting meat for meals, the nations depended on fishing, too.[13] Groups of men went on fishing trips that could last as long as a month.[14] Though early Iroquois ate many kinds of animals, they did not eat snakes because they believed they were connected to evil spirits.[15]

Animals also provided the Iroquois with material they used to make the things they needed. For example, parts of the bear had many uses. Bear hides were used as blankets. The Iroquois covered themselves in bear grease to protect against cold weather in the winter and insects in the summer.[16] Deer hides were used to make clothes, and antlers and bones were used to make tools. They even used deer brains to tan hides.[17] Nearly every part of the beaver was used. Its teeth made sharp tools and its large, flat tail contributed to delicious meals.[18]

Work was a time when people could come together to talk and

An Iroquois beaded hide dress

The Iroquois traveled by canoes made of elm bark like the one (far left) in this village.

share ideas. A group of men would chop down trees and take the logs to the village. Once there, they would cut up enough wood for each family and deliver it to their homes.[19] After years of living in the same area, villagers would take careful notice of when the area around their community was changing. Many of the animals had been hunted. The fruit and berries were picked. Women had planted and replanted the same place so often that crops refused to grow plentifully in the depleted soil. These signs helped the Iroquois see it was time to relocate. When the Iroquois relocated, their new village was developed close to the old one so men did not have to travel too far to clear the land and build new longhouses.[20] It took about two years for the men to rebuild a village.[21]

Seneca warriors fought with bows and arrows, clubs, shields, and spears.

Warriors

Early Iroquois people believed men and boys should be strong warriors. Males who were brave and successful warriors were respected. One scholar explains that a male's "success in battle increased [his] stature in his clan and village. His prospects for [a good] marriage, his chances for recognition as a village leader, and his hopes for eventual selection [as a chief] depended largely—though by no means entirely—on his skill on the warpath."[22] Historically, the Senecas and the Mohawks were especially skilled at warfare and were feared by many.

Iroquois Clothing

Clothing and shoes were made from the hides of such animals as deer, moose, and elk. To make clothes warm, the Iroquois used beaver, bear, and wolf fur.[23] Some clothes were made out of plant materials. Men wore breechcloth made from deerskin. Women wore skirts

Iroquois ceremonial dancers

and dresses. Men and women wore tunics, leggings, and moccasins. A Dutch preacher named Johannes Megapolensis, Jr. wrote the following in his journal in 1664 about how the Mohawks dressed.

> In winter, they hang about them simply an undressed deer or bear or panther skin; or they take some beaver and otter skins, wild cat, raccoon, martin, otter, mink, squirrel or such like skins, which are plenty in this country, and sew some of them to others, until it is a square piece, and that is then a garment for them; or they buy of us Dutchmen two and a half ells of duffel, and that they hang simply about them, just as it was torn off, without sewing it, and walk away with it. They look at themselves constantly, and think they are very fine. They make themselves stockings and also shoes of deer skin, or they take leaves of their corn, and plait them together and use them for shoes.[24]

Today, the Iroquois only wear traditional clothing during special ceremonies.[25]

The Midwinter Festival began with people
wearing "Big Head" masks made of corn husks.

CHAPTER 4
BELIEFS

The Iroquois believe all things have spirits, including animals, rocks, and land. These spirits can be helpful or harmful. Scholars say spirits of the field were "acknowledged and shown respect."[1] Giving thanks to the Creator for land was important. Long ago, the Iroquois began offering tobacco and other valuables to the spirits on a daily basis.

Trees were significant. Certain ones served as religious symbols. For example, the pine tree symbolized "the lasting strength of the Great League."[2]

Celebrations

Women arranged many celebrations and ceremonies throughout the year. Some festivals were designed to give thanks to different people, such as ancestors. Others showed gratitude for things, including the sun and the moon. Celebrations often included music. Drums, wooden courting flutes, and rattles were played.[3] Festivals usually did not begin until the clan mother arrived.[4]

The Midwinter Festival was held in January to give thanks to the Creator and the spirits. The festival included dream guessing, an activity that allowed one person to share part of a dream while the others tried to guess its meaning and give the dreamer the object he dreamed about.[5]

Special ceremonies were held to show respect to the earth in the spring, too. The Thunder Ceremony was held when rain was needed.[6] This ceremony involved men playing lacrosse with a wooden ball and a stick.

Feasts were also important celebrations with religious meaning. Some feasts were given to calm the spirits. For example, a curing feast was given when a family member contracted an illness, followed by a thanksgiving feast if the person recovered.[7] Many of these celebrations and ceremonies are still held today.

False Face Societies

Traditionally, the nations had religious societies or groups. For example,

False face mask

the false face societies were made up of people who said they could heal the sick and make sense of their dreams. The name comes from the masks they wore while healing people or while participating in special ceremonies. Researchers say "men become members of this society when they dream of . . . [an] ancestor who has piercing eyes, and frequently a bent nose and crooked mouth."[8] To get his mask, the dreamer described his dream to an artist and that person carved the mask. Most masks were red and black. False face societies still exist today, and they are important for many of the ceremonies that take place throughout the year.[9]

Christian Religions

People who believed in Christian religions went to the Iroquois to convert members of the

Wooden Kateri Tekakwitha statue

six nations. For example, the French brought Roman Catholicism to Iroquois communities during the 1600s. Kateri Tekakwitha was among the many who became Catholic. When Kateri was eleven years old, her uncle told her to assist three priests. It was during this time that Kateri might have begun to adopt Catholic beliefs. By her teen years, she developed a strong Catholic faith and refused to be married. Once she converted to Catholicism, Kateri was named Catherine.[10] She died a few years later.

After Kateri's death, people noticed special things about her. Priests pointed out a miracle that took place while they prayed over Kateri's body—the scars on her face disappeared. She was nominated for sainthood in 1884. This meant Kateri could someday be recognized as holy, or godly. Catholics who were ill began to pray to Kateri, and they were healed. On October 21, 2012, Kateri Tekakwitha became the first Native American saint.[11]

Like Handsome Lake, Cornplanter, the Iroquois warrior pictured here, belonged to the Wolf Clan.

Another well-known figure, Handsome Lake, inspired others to worship in a new way. Handsome Lake was a Seneca who combined many Iroquois ways of worshiping the Creator with ideas inspired by the Quaker religion.[12] Handsome Lake's ideas became popular between 1800 and 1815.[13] He preached that the Iroquois should avoid alcohol, witchcraft, and greed.[14] Handsome Lake's teachings are called the Code of Handsome Lake. Today, some Iroquois still worship based on Handsome Lake's ideas.[15]

Kateri Tekakwitha
(1656–1680)

Kateri Tekakwitha is sometimes called the Lily of the Mohawk.[16] Her father, Kenneronkwa, was a Mohawk. Her mother, Kahenta, an Algonquin-speaking Indian, became a part of the Mohawk nation after being captured by the Mohawks around 1653. Kenneronkwa and Kahenta had two children. Kateri was born in 1656. Four years later, smallpox killed many in her village, including her parents and brother. The disease left Kateri's face badly scarred and ruined her eyesight. Orphaned, she moved in with her aunt and uncle. Kateri's uncle, a chief, was not fond of Roman Catholic people who tried to convert the Iroquois.[17]

Kateri Tekakwitha painting, 1690

Kateri became Catholic, but her family did not approve. She eventually left home and settled in a Catholic Indian settlement in Canada. While there, she prayed for hours, kneeling in the snow, and ate very little. Kateri did this because she wanted to express her faith in God. She became ill and died at the young age of twenty-four.[18]

Some Iroquois question whether Kateri actually existed. Others believe the priest who wrote about her did not tell the truth. Still, others are proud Kateri became Catholic.[19]

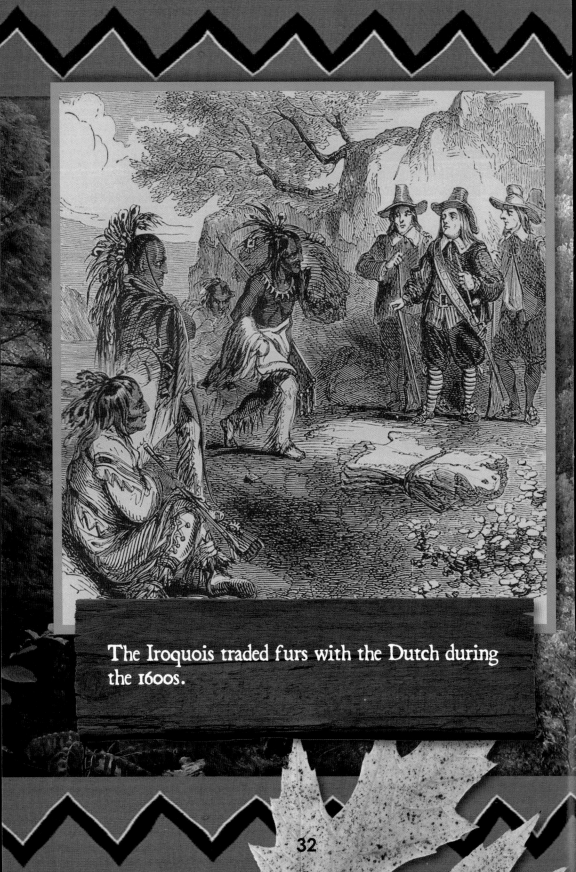

The Iroquois traded furs with the Dutch during the 1600s.

CHAPTER 5
EUROPEAN CONTACT
AND BEYOND

Some scholars say that when Europeans arrived in North America, there were about 100,000 Iroquois speakers living in present-day New York State and the southern part of Quebec and Ontario, Canada. The Iroquois population decreased after Europeans arrived.[1]

During the 1600s, the Iroquois developed a strong business relationship with the Dutch. The Dutch gave the Iroquois copper pots, iron axes, guns, knives, metal, cloth, wampum, cooking pots, and kettles. The Iroquois gave the Dutch fur. Animal fur was used to make hats that were popular in Europe. When the Dutch were driven out of the area, the English settled in and the nations traded with them instead.

Before long, the Iroquois controlled fur trading, but two problems became obvious by 1640. First, they had hunted most of the beavers near their villages. Second, the Iroquois did not have the type of beaver fur that most European traders wanted. Soon the French, the Huron, the Neutral, the Erie, Algonquin-speaking tribes in the Saint Lawrence River region in Canada, and the six nations were all competing for thick fur pelts to trade. Eager to solve their problem of scarce beaver pelts, the Iroquois attacked canoes with beaver furs bound for trading posts.[2]

Europeans called this struggle to maintain control of the fur trade the Beaver Wars of 1649–1654.[3]

Years earlier, the Dutch had given the Iroquois firearms. The Iroquois did not hesitate to use them. Iroquois warriors with guns had an unfair advantage over other nations interested in trading. Also, weapons such as flint arrowheads were being made from iron, copper, and brass and could pierce traditional Indian wooden armor. This greatly increased the risk of death.[4] The Iroquois used their weapons and skill at warfare to control the waterways from the St. Lawrence River in New York to Tennessee and from Maine to Michigan.[5] Many nation members and colonists lost their lives.

Relating to Europeans

The relationship between the Iroquois and Europeans was a complex one. The Iroquois enjoyed using European goods acquired through trading, but the European presence disrupted their way of life. Many Iroquois died in battle, but thousands also died from European diseases, such as measles, smallpox, and influenza. All of the nations were affected. Numerous Mohawks died from diseases in 1647 and 1673; the Onondaga suffered from 1656 to 1657; smallpox killed many of the Oneida, Onondaga, Cayuga, and Seneca from 1661 to 1663; and the Seneca suffered from diseases again in 1668 and 1676.[6] European diseases were new to the Iroquois, and people living there did not have natural immunity to fight the illnesses.

Though the Iroquois befriended some Europeans, others became enemies. Settlers tried to take land from the Iroquois, which sparked more wars. Some Iroquois fled to Canada and other areas in northern New York. Others stayed and made decisions about how to exist alongside European colonists.

American Revolution

At first, the nations tried to remain neutral when the colonists had disagreements with others. This grew difficult during the Revolutionary War. The war took place after colonists decided to unite and fight for independence from Britain. Grand Council meetings gave chiefs from each nation the opportunity to discuss important issues. If all of the nations did not agree about something, each nation was free to make its own decision about the matter.

Clan mothers and women in general were persuasive. They shared their opinions about war with others, including chiefs. During the Revolutionary War, a Mohawk clan mother called Molly Brant encouraged the Mohawk to support the British cause. The Seneca and Onondaga nations also decided to support the British.[7] Some sources say the Cayuga remained neutral.[8] After lengthy discussions, the Oneida and Tuscarora nations supported the American colonists. The disagreement about the Revolutionary War caused problems among the nations.[9]

British General Burgoyne secured an alliance with Native Americans during the American Revolutionary War.

Before long, the six nations were fighting each other in a war they had wanted to avoid.

American colonists were unhappy because most of the nations sided with the British. In 1779, General George Washington sent American forces to destroy Iroquois territory. Forty Iroquois towns were ruined, and soldiers burned cornfields filled with over 160,000 bushels of corn.[10] Without homes and food, many moved to Fort Niagara in New York.

Angry soldiers, including Red Jacket, Joseph Brant, and Cornplanter, Iroquois warriors faithful to the British, led attacks against the American colonists and the Oneida and Tuscarora.[11] The Iroquois, American colonists, and the British suffered and lost loved ones.

After the Revolutionary War, the Iroquois were told they could move back to their land in New York if they would sell some of it. Iroquois leaders refused. Before the war, Iroquois nations owned most of New York State. They held the title to about four-fifths of the total area.[12]

Joseph Brant

Warriors like Joseph Brant and Cornplanter did not receive land from the British as they were promised. Instead, they received some land in Canada. Many Iroquois led by Joseph Brant relocated to the Grand River Reservation in Ontario, Canada, in 1785. A reservation is land reserved for Native Americans. Once in Canada, the Iroquois established another confederacy. Now there was one in Canada and one in New York.[13]

American leaders attempted to make peace with the Iroquois. They suggested a treaty. The Iroquois signed the Treaty of Fort Stanwix of 1784.[14] The Fort Stanwix Treaty says the Iroquois and the United States agree to divide lands and be peaceful toward each other. To reward the Oneida and Tuscarora nations, American leaders allowed them to keep their land.[15]

The United States did not honor the Treaty of Fort Stanwix. In 1785, a year after the treaty was signed, New York State got 300,000 acres of Oneida land for $11,500. A few years later, in 1788, the state got almost five million acres of Oneida lands.[16] The Oneida began to leave their home in New York. One researcher maintains that "by 1855, only 161 Oneidas were counted in the state census."[17] Many moved to Wisconsin. Others settled on the Onondaga Reservation in New York. Americans also encouraged the other nations to give up most of their land in exchange for very little money and goods, such as tools, cloth, and guns.

Six Nations Now
With only a few acres of land left, the Iroquois lost some of their freedom. They could not fish, hunt, or farm as freely as they had in the past. These changes impacted how Iroquois men worked. Many began to look outside their communities for jobs. Some Mohawks found work as steelworkers in 1886, and helped build many important bridges and buildings, such as the Quebec Bridge in Canada and the Rockefeller Center and Empire State Building in New York. Though the work is dangerous, many Mohawks continue to construct bridges and skyscrapers throughout the United States.[18]

The six nations continue to thrive. They are still fighting to get their land back, and they have opened businesses on some of it. For example, the Cayuga own an ice cream stand and miniature golf course, a farm stand, and an auto repair shop.[19] The Seneca nation owns casinos, convenience stores, and construction businesses.[20]

Iroquois nations own seven reservations in New York State and one in Wisconsin. Modern Iroquois also live on reservations in Canada whereas others do not live on reservations at all. Wherein the six nations used to live together in villages, they now live in different parts of the United States, Canada, and areas throughout the world.[21] Despite this, they maintain the Iroquois Confederacy.[22] The Iroquois modern government is called the Six Nations.

Clans remain strong, and the Grand Council continues to consist of the Elder Brothers (Mohawk nation and Seneca nation), the Younger Brothers (Oneida nation, Tuscarora nation, and Cayuga nation), and one Firekeeper (Onondaga nation).[23] Iroquois tradition and history is still preserved, practiced, and celebrated.

The Iroquois consist of six nations that form the Iroquois Confederacy. They are admired for bravery, democracy, and agriculture.

Wampum

Wampum are shell beads that are strung together. They appear in Iroquois mythology and history. In the story of the Iroquois Confederacy, Hiawatha discovers wampum in a pond and uses it to make a belt. In other stories, wampum is magical.[24] Throughout history, wampum has been used in mourning rituals, to recall ideas, and to record the details of a treaty, agreement, or promise.[25]

wampum shells

Since the shells were found by people who lived near coastal waters in New England and Long Island, New York, the Iroquois often acquired wampum through trading. The Iroquois excelled at wampum trading during the fur trade in the mid-1600s. Some scholars say wampum was even used as money.[26] In 1664, Reverend Johannes Megapolensis Jr. observed the Mohawk and wrote the following in his journal.

> *Their money consists of certain little bones, made of shells or cockles, which are found on the sea-beach; a hole is drilled through the middle of the little bones, and these they string upon thread, or they make of them belts as broad as a hand, or broader, and hang them on their necks, or around their bodies. They have also several holes in their ears, and there they likewise hang some. They value these little bones as highly as many Christians do gold, silver and pearls; but they do not like our money, and esteem it no better than iron.*

The Iroquois are trying to regain many of their historical objects, like wampum belts, from museums that have put them on display. The Onondaga were the Keepers of the League Wampums. Wampum belts are now held by chiefs in Onondaga, New York, and Grand River in Canada.

1. Some scholars think the United States based its democratic system on the Iroquois Grand Council. Just as with the Iroquois, U.S. leaders are chosen by the people. Clan mothers select chiefs, but the entire clan must support their choices in order to proceed.

2. Storytelling (customarily done at nighttime), giving speeches, and persuasion are important parts of the Iroquois oral tradition.

3. Iroquois women owned and made decisions about land during a time when white women were not allowed to do so. Inspired by Iroquois women, many women's rights leaders, such as Elizabeth Cady Stanton and Lucretia Mott fought for equal rights, including the right to vote.

4. The word *wampum* comes from an Algonquin phrase that means "strings of white." Wampum were important white or purple shells. The white shells came from hard clams, and the purple shells came from whelks or mollusks. Researchers believe the white symbolized purity and the purple stood for grief. Sometimes the beads were dyed red to indicate war. Nearly everything about wampum belts symbolized something, and historians can read the messages on the belts.

5. When the Iroquois adopted Christianity, they included their own beliefs about the Creator.

6. Iroquois men sometimes put tribal tattoos on their faces and bodies whereas women did not.

7. When there was snow on the ground, the Iroquois would use snowshoes and sleds to travel across land.

8. At first, armor-clad Iroquois warriors fought with bows and arrows, clubs, and spears. Later, they fought with guns.

9. By 1666, the Iroquois traded their armor for a simple loincloth and for a pair of moccasins. Armor did not prevent gunshot wounds. Light clothing allowed fighters to move easily and quickly in battle.

10. The Iroquois filled drums with water. The sound of each drum differed based on the amount of water inside.

Chapter 1. Iroquois Confederacy

1. *Realm of the Iroquois* (Alexandria, VA: Time-Life Books, 1993), p. 25.

2. Loretta Hall, "Iroquois Confederacy," Countries and Their Cultures, http://www.everyculture.com/multi/Ha-La/Iroquois-Confederacy.html

3. Arthur C. Parker, "The Origin of the Iroquois as Suggested by Their Archeology," *American Anthropologist,* New Series 18, no. 4 (1916), p. 482. JSTOR accessed September 29, 2012.

4. Thomas V. Peterson, "Iroquois Confederacy," *Religions of the World: A Comprehensive Encyclopedia of Beliefs and Practices,* edited by J. Gordon Melton and Martin Baumann, 2nd ed., vol. 4 (Santa Barbara, CA: ABC-CLIO, 2010), p. 1508. *Gale Virtual Reference Library* accessed September 27, 2012.

5. Douglas George-Kanentiio, "Peace Practices among the Iroquois," *Religion East & West,* no. 10 (2010), p. 121.

6. "Birth of a Nation—Relations With Our Brothers: 1613 to Today," Onondaga Nation: People of the Hills, http://www.onondaganation.org/aboutus/history.html

7. Thomas V. Peterson, "Iroquois Confederacy," pp. 1507–1509.

8. *Realm of the Iroquois,* p. 25.

9. Robert E. Powless, "Iroquois," *World Book Encyclopedia,* vol. 10 (Chicago: World Book, 2009), p. 453.

10. Bruce Johansen, "Dating the Iroquois Confederacy," *Akwesasne Notes,* 1, no. 3–4 (1995), p. 62.

11. Ibid.

12. Michael Johnson, *Tribes of the Iroquois Confederacy* (Great Britain: Osprey Publishing, 2003), p. 22, http://www.ospreypublishing.com/store/book.aspx?bookcode=s4906

13. W. M. Beauchamp, "Iroquois Women," *The Journal of American Folklore* 13, no. 49 (1900), p. 90.

14. Jan Noel, "Fertile with Fine Talk: Ungoverned Tongues among Haudenosaunee Women and Their Neighbors," *Ethnohistory* 57, no. 2 (2010), p. 203. JSTOR accessed November 29, 2012.

15. Leonard J. Sadosky, "Iroquois League," *Encyclopedia of the American Revolution: Library of Military History,* ed. Harold E. Selesky. vol. 1 (Detroit: Charles Scribner's Sons, 2006), pp. 557–559. *Gale Virtual Reference Library* accessed September 27, 2012.

16. *Realm of the Iroquois,* p. 13.

Chapter 2. Community

1. *Realm of the Iroquois* (Alexandria, VA: Time-Life Books, 1993), pp. 2–17.

2. Ibid., p. 34.

3. Loretta Hall, "Iroquois Confederacy," Countries and Their Cultures, http://www.everyculture.com/multi/Ha-La/Iroquois-Confederacy.html

4. *Realm of the Iroquois,* p. 34.

5. Ibid., p. 13.

6. "Facts," Onodaga Nation: People of the Hills, http://www.onondaganation.org/aboutus/facts.html

7. "Iroquois Confederacy," *Columbia Electronic Encyclopedia,* 6th Edition, November 2011, pp. 1–2. Academic Search Complete, Ebscohost accessed November 20, 2012.

8. Hall, "Iroquois Confederacy," Countries and Their Cultures.

9. *Realm of the Iroquois,* p. 35.

10. Douglas George-Kanentiio, "Peace Practices among the Iroquois," *Religion East & West,* no. 10 (2010), p. 123.

11. William A. Starna and José António Brandão, "From the Mohawk-Mohican War to the Beaver Wars," *Ethnohistory,* 51, no. 4 (2004), p. 729. JSTOR accessed September 29, 2012.

12. Bruce Johansen, "Dating the Iroquois Confederacy," *Akwesasne Notes,* 1, no. 3–4 (1995), p. 2.

13. Tuscarora and Six Nations Web Sites. http://tuscaroras.com/

14. "Clans," Seneca Nation of Indians: Keeper of the Western Door, http://sni.org/culture/clans/
15. George-Kanentiio, "Peace Practices among the Iroquois," p. 122.

Chapter 3. Daily Life
1. W. M. Beauchamp, "Iroquois Women," *The Journal of American Folklore* 13, no. 49 (1900), p. 81.
2. *Realm of the Iroquois* (Alexandria, VA: Time-Life Books, 1993), p. 28.
3. Ibid., p. 36.
4. "Culture," Seneca Nation of Indians: Keeper of the Western Door, http://sni.org/culture/
5. Beauchamp, "Iroquois Women," p. 82.
6. William N. Fenton, *The Great Tree and the Longhouse: A Political History of the Iroquois Confederacy* (Norman, OK: University of Oklahoma Press, 1998), p. 11.
7. *Realm of the Iroquois*, p. 42.
8. Loretta Hall, "Iroquois Confederacy," Countries and Their Cultures, http://www.everyculture.com/multi/Ha-La/Iroquois-Confederacy.html
9. Ibid.
10. Ibid.
11. *Realm of the Iroquois*, p. 29.
12. Ibid., p. 38.
13. Ibid., p. 30.
14. Ibid.
15. Ibid., p. 38.
16. Ibid., p. 28.
17. Ibid., p. 29.
18. Ibid.
19. Beauchamp, "Iroquois Women," p. 82.
20. *Realm of the Iroquois*, p. 37.
21. Hall, "Iroquois Confederacy," Countries and Their Cultures.
22. Daniel K. Richter, "War and Culture: The Iroquois Experience," *The William and Mary Quarterly,* Third Series 40, no. 4 (1983), p. 530.
23. Iroquois Indian Museum, http://www.iroquoismuseum.org

24. Johannes Megapolensis, Jr., "A Short Account of the Mohawk Indians," *Short Account of the Mohawk Indians* (January 10, 2009), p. 168. Academic Search Complete, EBSCOhost accessed November 29, 2012.
25. Iroquois Indian Museum, http://www.iroquoismuseum.org

Chapter 4. Beliefs
1. *Realm of the Iroquois* (Alexandria, VA: Time-Life Books, 1993), p. 38.
2. Ibid., p. 28.
3. Loretta Hall, "Iroquois Confederacy," Countries and Their Cultures, http://www.everyculture.com/multi/Ha-La/Iroquois-Confederacy.html
4. "Facts," Onondaga Nation: People of the Hills, http://www.onondaganation.org/aboutus/facts.html
5. Hall, "Iroquois Confederacy," Countries and Their Cultures.
6. Michael Johnson, *Tribes of the Iroquois Confederacy* (Great Britain: Osprey Publishing, 2003), p. 23, http://www.ospreypublishing.com/store/book.aspx?bookcode=s4906
7. *Realm of the Iroquois,* p. 38.
8. Thomas V. Peterson, "Iroquois Confederacy," *Religions of the World: A Comprehensive Encyclopedia of Beliefs and Practices,* edited by J. Gordon Melton and Martin Baumann, 2nd ed., vol. 4 (Santa Barbara, CA: ABC-CLIO, 2010), p. 1508. *Gale Virtual Reference Library* accessed September 27, 2012.
9. Ibid.
10. "Kateri Tekakwitha." *Encyclopedia of World Biography,* Vol. 23 (Detroit: Gale, 2003). Gale Biography In Context accessed November, 29 2012.; "Kateri Tekakwitha." *Notable Native Americans.* Gale, 1995. Gale Biography In Context. Web. Accessed November 29, 2012.
11. Sharon Otterman, "Complex Emotions Over First American Indian Saint." *New York Times,* July 25, 2012: A21(L).

Gale Biography In Context. Web. Accessed November 29, 2012.; also Alyssa Newcomb, "Kateri Tekakwitha Becomes First American Indian Saint," http://abcnews.go.com/blogs/headlines/2012/10/kateri-tekakwitha-becomes-first-american-indian-saint/

12. Douglas George-Kanentiio, "Peace Practices among the Iroquois," *Religion East & West,* no. 10 (2010), p. 121.

13. Arthur C. Parker, "The Origin of the Iroquois as Suggested by Their Archeology," *American Anthropologist,* New Series 18, no. 4 (1916), p. 481. JSTOR accessed September 29, 2012.

14. Peterson, "Iroquois Confederacy," p. 1508.

15. Iroquois Indian Museum, http://www.iroquoismuseum.org

16. *Realm of the Iroquois,* p. 96.

17. "Kateri Tekakwitha," *Encyclopedia of World Biography;* "Kateri Tekakwitha," *Notable Native Americans.*

18. Ibid.

19. "Kateri Tekakwitha," *Notable Native Americans.*

Chapter 5. European Contact and Beyond

1. *Realm of the Iroquois* (Alexandria, VA: Time-Life Books, 1993), p. 24.

2. Daniel K. Richter, "War and Culture: The Iroquois Experience," *The William and Mary Quarterly,* Third Series 40, no. 4 (1983), p. 539.

3. *Realm of the Iroquois,* p. 81.

4. Richter, "War and Culture," p. 538.

5. Robert E. Powless, "Iroquois," *World Book Encyclopedia,* Vol. 10 (Chicago: World Book, 2009), p. 453.

6. Richter, "War and Culture," p. 537.

7. Leonard J. Sadosky, "Iroquois League," *Encyclopedia of the American Revolution: Library of Military History,* ed. Harold E. Selesky. Vol. 1 (Detroit: Charles Scribner's Sons, 2006), pp. 557–559. *Gale Virtual Reference Library* accessed September 27, 2012.

8. Cayuga Nation: People of the Great Swamp, http://www.cayuganation-nsn.gov

9. Loretta Hall, "Iroquois Confederacy," Countries and Their Cultures, http://www.everyculture.com/multi/Ha-La/Iroquois-Confederacy.html

10. Sadosky, "Iroquois League."

11. Ibid.

12. Doug George-Kanentiio, "How Much Land Did the Iroquois Possess?" *Akwesasne Notes* 1, no. 3–4 (1995), p. 60.

13. *Realm of the Iroquois,* p. 141.

14. Sadosky, "Iroquois League."

15. "Treaties," Seneca Nation of Indians: Keeper of the Western Door, http://sni.org/culture/treaties/

16. Laurence M. Hauptman, "The Iroquois Indians and the Rise of the Empire State: Ditches, Defense, and Dispossession," *New York History* 79, no. 4 (1998), p. 336.

17. Hauptman, "The Iroquois Indians and the Empire State," p. 351.

18. *Realm of the Iroquois,* p. 163.

19. Cayuga Nation: People of the Great Swamp, http://www.cayuganation-nsn.gov/

20. Seneca Nation of Indians: Keeper of the Western Door, http://sni.org/

21. Hall, "Iroquois Confederacy," Countries and Their Cultures.

22. Ibid.

23. George-Kanentiio, "Peace Practices," p. 125.

24. Fenton, *Longhouse,* p. 226.

25. Hall, "Iroquois Confederacy," Countries and Their Cultures.

26. Fenton, *Longhouse,* pp. 224–225.

Books

Dolbear, Emily J. and Peter Benoit. *The Iroquois* (True Books). New York: Scholastic, 2003.

Duden, Jane. *The Iroquois: The Six Nations Confederacy.* Mankato, MN: Capstone, 2007.

Graymont, Barbara. *The Iroquois: Indians of North America.* New York: Chelsea House Publishers, 2005.

Johansen, Bruce. *The Iroquois: The History & Culture of Native Americans.* New York: Facts on File, 2010.

Works Consulted

Abler, Thomas S. "The Great Law and the Longhouse: A Political History of the Iroquois Confederacy." *Ethnohistory* 47, no. 2 (2000). *Academic Search Complete,* EBSCOhost (accessed December 1, 2012).

Beauchamp, W. M. "Iroquois Women." *The Journal of American Folklore* 13, no. 49 (1900).

Cayuga Nation: People of the Great Swamp. http://www.cayuganation-nsn.gov/

Fenton, William N. *The False Faces of the Iroquois.* Norman: University of Oklahoma Press, 1987.

Fenton, William N. *The Great Tree and the Longhouse: A Political History of the Iroquois Confederacy.* Norman: University of Oklahoma Press, 1998.

George-Kanentiio, Douglas. "How Much Land Did the Iroquois Possess?" *Akwesasne Notes* 1, no. 3–4 (1995).

George-Kanentiio, Douglas. "Peace Practices among the Iroquois." *Religion East & West*, no. 10 (2010).

Hauptman, Laurence M. "The Iroquois Indians and the Rise of the Empire State: Ditches, Defense, and Dispossession." *New York History* 79, no. 4 (1998).

Hill, Loretta. "Iroquois Confederacy" Countries and Their Cultures. http://www.everyculture. com/multi/Ha-La/Iroquois-Confederacy.html.

"Iroquois Confederacy." *Columbia Electronic Encyclopedia,* 6th Edition (November 2011): 1–2. *Academic Search Complete,* EBSCOhost (accessed November 20, 2012).

Johansen, Bruce. "Dating the Iroquois Confederacy." *Akwesasne Notes* 1, no. 3–4 (1995), pp. 62–63.

"Kateri Tekakwitha." *Encyclopedia of World Biography.* Vol. 23. Detroit: Gale, 2003. *Gale Biography in Context.* Web (accessed November 29, 2012).

"Kateri Tekakwitha." *Notable Native Americans.* Gale, 1995. *Gale Biography In Context.* Web (accessed November 29, 2012).

Megapolensis, Johannes, Jr. "A Short Account of the Mohawk Indians." *Short Account Of The Mohawk Indians* 168 (2009). *Academic Search Complete,* EBSCOhost (accessed November 29, 2012).

Newcomb, Alyssa. "Kateri Tekakwitha Becomes First American Indian Saint." http://abcnews.go.com/blogs/headlines/2012/10/kateri-tekakwitha-becomes-first-american-indian-saint/

Noel, Jan. "Fertile with Fine Talk: Ungoverned Tongues among Haudenosaunee Women and Their Neighbors." *Ethnohistory* 57, no. 2 (2010). JSTOR (accessed November 29, 2012).

Onondaga Nation: People of the Hills. http://www.onondaganation.org/aboutus/history.html

Otterman, Sharon. "Complex Emotions Over First American Indian Saint." *New York Times*, July 25, 2012: A21(L) *Gale Biography In Context*. Web (accessed November 29, 2012).

Parker, Arthur C. "The Origin of the Iroquois as Suggested by Their Archeology." *American Anthropologist*, New Series, 18, no. 4 (October–December 1916). JSTOR (accessed September 29, 2012).

Peterson, Thomas V. "Iroquois Confederacy." In *Religions of the World: A Comprehensive Encyclopedia of Beliefs and Practices*, edited by J. Gordon Melton and Martin Baumann. 2nd ed. Vol. 4. Santa Barbara, CA: ABC-CLIO, 2010. *Gale Virtual Reference Library* (accessed September 27, 2012).

Powless, Robert E. "Iroquois." *World Book Encyclopedia*, Vol. 10. Chicago: World Book, 2009.

Realm of the Iroquois. Alexandria, VA: Time-Life Books, 1993.

Richter, Daniel K. "War and Culture: The Iroquois Experience." *The William and Mary Quarterly, Third Series*, 40, no. 4 (1983). JSTOR. (accessed November 29, 2012).

Sadosky, Leonard J. "Iroquois League." *Encyclopedia of the American Revolution: Library of Military History*. ed. Harold E. Selesky. Vol. 1. (Detroit: Charles Scribner's Sons, 2006, *Gale Virtual Reference Library* (accessed September 27, 2012).

Seneca Nation of Indians: Keeper of the Western Door. http://sni.org/culture/

Starna, William A. and José António Brandão. "From the Mohawk-Mohican War to the Beaver Wars." *Ethnohistory* 51, no. 4 (2004). JSTOR (accessed September 29, 2012).

Tuscarora and Six Nations Web Sites. http://tuscaroras.com/

On the Internet

Cayuga Nation of New York
    http://www.cayuganation-nsn.gov/
Haudenosaunee (Iroquois) Indian Fact Sheet
    http://www.bigorrin.org/iroquois_kids.htm
Iroquois Indian Museum
    http://www.iroquoismuseum.org/index.html
Onondaga Nation: People of the Hills
    http://www.onondaganation.org/
Seneca Nation of Indians: Keeper of the Western Door
    http://www.sni.org

acquire—To gain.

ancestor—A relative who lived long ago.

convert—To change from one religious belief to another.

embroidery—Needle work done to decorate cloth.

mourn—To show sadness when someone dies.

myth—A traditional story that tries to explain mysterious events.

neutral—Taking no sides in an argument.

relocate—To move to a new location.

stature—Quality or status gained by doing something well.

symbol—Something that stands for something else.

MEET THE
AUTHOR

KaaVonia Hinton teaches in the College of Education at Old Dominion University, and is author of several books for children, including *Desegregating America's Schools*, *Jacqueline Woodson*, and *Brown v. Board of Education of Topeka, Kansas, 1954*.